☙knots❧

By

Susan Marie

PublishAmerica
Baltimore

First printing

At the specific preference of the author, PublishAmerica allowed this work to remain exactly as the author intended, verbatim, without editorial input.

ISBN: 1-4241-1912-X
PUBLISHED BY PUBLISHAMERICA, LLLP
www.publishamerica.com
Baltimore

Printed in the United States of America

☙ To Billy ❧

~ May you never lose sight ~

To Julia,
my sister
in spirit + blood
I love you
Susie
+

I would like to acknowledge my families, foremost, for providing me with skills essential to survival. Along with my own learning, they have each helped me to overcome difficulties, celebrate happiness, allow sadness, grieve, heal and grow.

To my friends, who watched me burst from a child to an adult, I thank you for believing in my writing and for many years of experience I shall never forget.

Waving to my fellow artists, poets, and writers who have not only taught me how to become a better person, but have guided me through extremely difficult times in my life by being there for me. To each of you, and you know who you are, my heart is full of gratitude for not only seeing me as a blossoming writer, but for guiding my writing and my spirit. Without any of you, this book would not be possible.

To Publish America, I am grateful. They chose to accept my thoughts, turning them into this. To everyone involved in the process, thank you for believing in me and taking a chance.

For our lost prophets. May they thrive forever in our souls.
Through their work, we survive.

To a most beautiful soul, who has brought me closer to myself.
By allowing me to fly, you taught me how to be free.

I love you and always shall.

~

Most importantly, to you, reading this right now. Thank you for picking it up.

Part I

Prelude

Awaken my love…

Denounce the quiet of your resolution
arising from a virgin dusting.
Consummated by the somber shadows of winter.

I have indulged myself for far too long.

Embracing the choir of your children,
tulip and daffodil,
buried within your bosom,
plumed in darkness.

Wailing, since the onset of frost.

Lift the veil.

Sing your sweetness
across the Eastern shore.
Let your voice echo in the valley,
migrating across our waters.

Brush your breath, fervid,
as an artist at his easel.
Heed the ice, my sentinel,
examine each crack and bleed
sailing, braids of gossamer, upon the wind.

Raise your voice, Sister!

Bid farewell, the Ice Princess.

Spread your palm, fingers splayed
upon her own, barren and glacial,
and lead her,
in love,

to paradise.

Madonna of the Rocks

illegitimate genius…

i
your kneeling figure

embossed
with monastery mirror

am draped for your study.

chiaroscuro,
your play of dark vs. light

Dearest Tuscany,

Does your proficiency suffice
when deciphering your son?

Verrocchio had laid his brush

he understood
such rusted knots
read backwards
through looking glass

before they needed
to be studied.

St. Jerome speaks,

beating his breast
to the sympathies of a lion

while John the Baptist looks on

emasculate.

The lap of Madonna
is burdened

a geometric precision
on rocks

the only grace,
an angel's gaze.

Gesso awash

in elegy.

Speech

How does one say

isleofview?

such words seem

hollow

pinging

echo like

stone

dropped for
distance

traveled

d
o
w
n

well(ing) within

Home

Knots

i want you to read me
poetry

you can watch my toes
curl
as flames
lick
from your skull

volts
zinginggggggg

this canvas
melting hues

a thousand gales
could not breathe

LIFE

yet one kiss

from your lips

has snapped
this mast

in two

Peine Forte Et Dure

wail,
your blackened tongue

lithe,
sharp as knives

prod me with whipcord

thumbs bound
behind my back
forced to speak
on my behalf
naught witness
to bear
in my defense

No Vacancy

~ FLASH ~

inside thine eyes

Draw my confession.

I choose to stand mute.

Sweet Cherry Bitters

Maya,
immaculate…

Come,
beneath canopy

erect

with buds
of
ivory

Complete profound transcendence
has left me quite attentive
to an unbridled awakening
from a deep, ontological sleep.

fell

with axe,
yeilded

Consummate
hearth

Relinquish this euphoric

weight

The grove of thy birth

Plaits

When you brush my hair
use long strokes
like sun rays
parting the sea

karma

is

shackled

at the base of my skull

Expel these sins

So we may skate
upon sea glass

a crystal ball

intact

a fuzzy rendition

of the last time
we met

Oak

Tilted slightly forward
kneeling,

your shadow
dances
before me

stars embroider themselves
on concentric cross-sections

oak
hard
wood

my palms
flat

in front of me.

Mea Culpa

Braids sway
slow motion

thrusting
deeper

the scourge,

still
the pooling…

Lips, purse
in silent quiver.

Kneeling,
in solemn pride.

I salvage

what
is
left.

Synthesis

It can be disputed,
that the dying breath
of man
is composed solely
of flushed, angelic breeze.

Not unlike
a delicate touch,
traversing each curve of hip
and thigh,
while lying, entwined
beneath a cool summer's morn'.

It can be disputed,
that such temperate breeze
resembles the joy felt
upon hearing an infant's first wail.

It has been proven,
that one's last breath
is nothing more
than carbon dioxide
and nutrients, dispelled.

I have seen more death than life.

I embody the bile
rising from the city's sewers.

Vomited,
from the cracked and bleeding mouths
of our forefathers.

The gutters ejaculate, stinging my skin,
pricking, as needles.

No matter how I try,
I cannot be scrubbed clean.

I dispute,
that death is anything pleasant.

For the living.

I have seen more death than life.

And I braid its bony fingers,
within my own.

In memory

~ Joseph Jacob Horvatits

Nevertheless

I saw you today,
scrolled within
the beard of a young man
as he thumbed through a magazine.

Curling burnt sienna
hugged his chin and
the seriousness of his gaze
into that text
reminded me of you.

I read Bukowski today
and there you were,
among the fuck you's
and the I love you's ~
while he beat his fingers bloody.

There you were,
lying beside his wife,
while simultaneously seeing
through his eyes
as her husband.

Kerouac even whispered your name
with a nonchalant wave of his hand,
explaining to me the difference
between exclaiming, "Man, I'm beat"
and just being tired.

I tasted you today.
You dissolved upon my tongue.

Rich toffee nut
settled into my throat
making my belly warm,
while Billie Holiday lamented
just how badly she needed a fix.

I saw you today,
oh yes, I did.

Everywhere I turned
there you were.

And My God,

it has left me quite sad.

Bloodink

Thought

a bubble
            burst

forgotten
cotton reams
of dreams

keenly carved
coiled spike

breach the flesh
within my chest

consume
my tomb

I beg of you

resume
your deed

for me,

please.

Deliver me.

Pieta'

I have always envied Michelangelo.

Not that I have met him
but in my mind's eye,
I see David

standing

in all his glory.

His pectorals and abdominals

intact

and Mother Mary
cradling her son
frozen in time

an ice princess.

No one ever noticing

the woman

and the crows feet
that hide beside her eyes.

Word

Where are the wooden scepters
philosophers,
dejecters
of truth?

word is broken

battered and bleeding
like a dog in the street
left to live
alone

as he were born

and you raise your Crys ~
to this?
sum Evian pisspost and miss it
doesn't matter
we all thirst
my lips are cracked
throat hoarse
temples throb
from thinking too much
these days
are filled with daggers
driven deep
falling as snowflakes
children
wide-eyed in wonder
mouths open

pleading

I wanna take 'em each
tell 'em it's

OK

to be angry
and rant and scream
when yer Momma's a bitch
yellin' at the t.v. screen
'cuz Daddy ain't home

but he used ta be

Our backs are broken

Close your mouths, children
open your mind
read a book
look inside
smell the bind
and glue
run your fingers
down
the
spine

Life

it's there for you
to

BE

or **NOT**

its up to you

to **DIS**
arm
or be charmed
by the garbage dump lot
of lies
and lives

LOST

man…

ain't nuthin' but
hello and goodbye.

~ With respect to Saul Williams

Semper Libertas

My hands, I hold
to the harsh wind
raising arm to sky

palm open, creased

I smile

and release, upturned

a bird

to flight

Note to Eldridge

The world is hemophiliac.

Cries have been heard
from the thunder, my friends.
Years before we inhaled
our first stale breath
on this plane,
we exhaled sweet honey
from whence we came.

Vomiting our souls
into a dying sky,
creating rainclouds.

Have you ever wondered
exactly why, as a child,
the clouds seemed to take shape?

It was not childhood imagination.

Moreso, the embers of your spirit
and those before you.
Aimlessly floating
on a new path ~
to an old life ~
down a new road ~
past thicket and bramble,
reaching row upon row of rosegarden.

Sentinel,
soldiers at arms.

One time I saw the skull
of my forefathers' in the sky
and I deemed myself insane.

Oh, to be lying
upon the damp slumber of life!

The living grass speaking volumes of
Whitman
Blake
Kerouac
Malcolm
JFK
Einstein
Martin Luther
King
Jr.
would take you by the hand, today
and kneel with you in solemn prayer,
muddying his pantleg
to kiss the soil,
with you in tow.

The thin line, woven
between where worlds collide,
astounds me.

I try to relinquish
what and who I once was
in order to become
what I am to be.

It is not enough for me
to be sustained, merely,
by the definition of "existence"
when I possess the ability to fly.

What thin line separates
my hand from passing ~
lucid and glasslike,
through that wall of oppression
lined with
hate
love
greed
empathy
grief
happiness
to where I can actually begin to feel

LIFE

tingling up my arm,
to my heart,
escalating to my brain,
sparking neurons to regenerate
back to a time
when there may have been a Utopia?

The entire human race
ceased to exist
when it stopped listening
to itself.

The message was lost
when the Romans
wielded mallet and spike.

The disconcerting fact
is that they were only doing their job.

The world is hemophiliac.

Maybe one day, hence,
like woman,

it will cease to bleed.

~ With respect to Eldridge Cleaver

Harvest

. . . and I asked him then, “How have you come to desire the delicacies of a woman?”

My God, I thought, *he is beauty,* as light danced and played up and down his adam’s apple, jutting as he spoke,

“I have a taste for the finer things in life.” A smirk alive within his eyes,
“A woman is likened to a ripened fruit. They both grow to term, only to burst, viscid and sweet upon one’s lips.”

I felt my own hand wander to the bones protruding below my throat and laughed,
“Well, my love, it looks to me as if you have stumbled upon an orchard.”

La Maschera Viene

smother me with commedia
a latent Mardi Gras
i never saw
nor will

cloak my sight
in dust and ash

ivory tusks
protruding
beneath withered strips

entwined papier-mache'

maschera viene

speak to me in riddles
until i am blind

i do not wish
to see
further

Blood Tears

She cried

she cried

she cried

they snuck behind her
rolling in

busying herself with
pinks, blues and violet canvas
created
by the marina
from her smile
the dusk of day

until they struck

electric, contorted

a lover's touch

icicles rained
splashing my face
kissing my forehead

as I watched

voyeur

It was passion, unbridled

and the loneliest moment
of my life.

She

Forgotten heroes rambled
sitars and drumbeats
as you warmed my face today

I thought you had gone for good

Leaving me with your sister moon-child
and the gray damp of evening

Your children lie about you
a death tress

blanketing your body
in a psycheledic bridal gown

I would love to braid your hair

Just once

Or hold your hand

But all I have of you
is this day

Pangea

Before there was language
antiquated herbivores roamed

we fed them greenery
waiting for the Earth to cool

to form itself

Somewhere inside of me
resides this memory
of a child, lost
yet not forgotten

Upon my hand, the scent
right palm speaking
of underbrush and silt

Exactly how it smells after a rainfall…

The fireside smoke
spirals
calling us home

the place of our birth

Strength of Strings

Through withered leaves
of rose and tree
lined paths do drift

and meet stirring
rising beneath the sky

Egress, to a way around
the stinging thorns
and snatching branches
that try to bar

A cord thus drawn
from wrist to hand
and hand to wrist

and back again

four points crossed
with silken twine
to bind thy soul for evermore

two hands, now joined
to tempt the fates
that would dare to test

the strength of strings

Rise to Babylon

Isaiah shouted,
"The daughter of Zion
has been left,
putrefied -
to the machinery
that once inhabited
the Mount."

Jesus was there, he took his last meal
and prayed:

Return to my Fathers' table,
the breast of my Mother.

Return to Babylon.

I am that daughter,
who knelt by His side
when he bled sand,
unable to beget blood.

Jesus needed a Hell's Angel
on his shoulder.

Our sons and daughters
are sent
blind faith
by Herod, resurrected.

Listen...

the Serenity Prayer
whispered
in restless slumber.

There are no prophets.

I am a bastard child of the New World.

Part II

Isaiah

I.

Thought
a beetle,

burrowed deep within these sockets
now a skull

hallowed.

My body,
porcelain

mask of lone spirit ~
rose and fumbled
from this innate

twitching.

Then I saw her...

Beneath line of sight
glinting off crest,
sparking the corner of my
eye.

Electric surreal concentric pools.

I bathed in her beauty

cleansed by my breath,
inhaling her own.

An exchange of Man and Earth.

Three souls bound to one.

II.

Naked and bestial,
I stood before her.

Eyes, downcast ~

In shame of my… misgivings.

Lavender and clover, minted
lifted my chin.

As butterscotch
fell from her eyes,
melting to the floor,
outlining curve
of breast and thigh.

Melding my feet
to my heart.

Entwined within her arms ~

I cried.

III.

I awoke
third day of my journey
to myself.

Imprints of last eve
upon pillow.

I reached with my hand, trembling.

She was but a dream.

Salt stung my eyes,
perspiring brow
dripping,
with the scent of us.

I recalled then
scoffing at her freedom,
and a frown
that had replaced her smile.

Oh, what a fool
this early on!

I have crushed
that which I love,
with my selfish want
of her everything.

And to me,
she gave so freely.

IV.

Attempting to regain
composure,

split second flight
of hummingbird
resounded, a thousand fold

Hence, the garden from which it came.

Song of angelic choir.

Kneeling in fresh sod
rescuing blooms
from strangling weeds,
she appeared.

Cheeks blushed bright
as the roses she tended.

I knew then,

we had become three.

V.

My heart gladdened
as I gazed.

Her beauty permeated
the air I now breathed,
radiating
sun
to light my day

Her hands, worn
yet tender to touch,
held my face
as I knelt beside her.

She lay with me.

Naked in our unity,
arms held high
thanking the skies

for breath.

VI.

I awoke this time
rejoicing my good fortune.

Constant rumblings below
led me to my hunt.

Taking arrow and bow,
I looked back over my shoulder
to my future,
and smiled.

She waved to me then,
smiling herself.

While each
sole
imprinted sacred forest bed.

It was there, I hunched,
heart beating, rapid.

Drawing back in fear
in awe,
of this beast before me ~
eyes narrowing,
I withdrew.

Together we feasted
on this precious breast.

And with each mouthful of bounty
we thanked the heavens
for the blessings of the Earth.

VII.

She beckoned to me then.

Hands resting, protective
upon soft, slow rise of belly
and motioned,
with finger hushed to lips.

To the fields, yonder.

Wheat towered above laurel
preceding vineyards, vast and silent.

Rows of neatly planted corn.
A backdrop to this canvas.
I looked down then
at my own hands.

And gazed again
at the men.
Slaving in the sun,
relentless.

My heart burst
from the echoes in the valley.

Through their songs of freedom.

VIII.

She held my palm
within her own,
now torn
by brush and bramble.

Stale breath of midday sun
darkened her vibrant pallor.

I wondered if it had been days since I had noticed.

She looked to me, with love
and I returned this gift
upon lips of berry,
kissed.

And it was then
the shine within her eye,
grew dim.

A lone tear fell
from granite pools.

Dropping to my palm.
Salt stinging fresh workday wounds.

I held her to me,
and this time ~

she cried.

I pretended as if
I did not notice

the weight of child, lost.

I held her frail frame
to my own.

And my agony
hidden,

deep within my throat.

IX.

We then fell before
a knarled twist of fate.

Locked within
each ancient limb,
long begotten tales of men
spoke to me.

My love sought solace
spreading tapestry
to lie her troubled brow.

I joined her then,
her hand with my own.

We became distracted
by the intricate design
of each branch,
a spider web.

A maze of arms and legs
entangled.
Reaching to me,
in embrace.

With great sorrow,
I held axe in hand.

And began to build our home,
upon the birthplace

of the Joshua Tree.

X.

Resilient raiment,
a sackcloth ~
draped my bottom half.

Allowing my chest, bare.
Each breast, rising as hills.

My ribcage.
A wishbone of youth,
outlined ripples, prominent ~
as the river raging before me.

My skin, sullied and olive,
darkened by the dying sun,
gifted me with masculinity.

I was pure in my birth.

On bent knee,
crushing rubble as I did,
the blinded eyes of man
embedded my skin,
now bleeding sin.
For the failures
of those before me.

I heaved a sigh,
gazing upon my creation.

A home,
for my love and I.

We disrobed
in our purity.

XI.

I found myself
next morning
enveloped
within stalks, luscious.

And turned to a basket,
weaved from flax and wicker.

It was birthing seed, unborn.

Fruit and vegetable
of weed and worry
strewn hapless within this berth,
the basket.

My hands, lumber
dove into this luxurious sea.

I filled my satchel.

Sifting good seed
from bad.

XII.

A delicate hand
then took hold of my shoulder,
startling me from my fury.

It was the woman.

She looked to me
not with shame,
but confusion.

Pointing northward
towards a farmhouse,
I understood.

I must repay this gift,
a penance.

For one raw bounty,
became my beast.

XIII.

The journey back to our
shelter
started that beetle

twitching.

And I saw the woman
ahead of me,
deep within her own pain.

She has given me a most precious gift.

Within her freedom,
I have found myself.

And within my eyes,
she has seen the woman she has been.

The one she shall grow to be.

XIV.

I found her
later that evening,
sprawled about
the foot of our bed.

Her body, pristine.

A fine meal.

And I took
and ate of her.

And she fed
as that of a woman,
starved.

XV.

At break of day,
a weight
lay beside me.

A single ray smiled
through harried roof,
to shine upon letters.

Silver gilt.

Sitting up,
I looked for my love
and heard nothing.

No clatter of dish or cup.
No feet, barefoot
slapping upon floor of sod.

I was alone.

I took this book
embossed,
as a cup to my lips
of fine wine.

Aged and sacred.

The corners were worn.

And with each creak of binding,
I read her heart.

Blood ink

I sensed her footfalls,
and retreated to slumber.

XVI.

A tress of ravens wings
came to me then,
in a dream.

Her wings brushed my cheeks
and she turned to me,
pointing a finger.

Onward.

There lie a forest,
Lush with pine and oak.

Three paths before me.

A road of twig and moss
to the right, bending East.

The second, fallen leaves and holly
straining Westward.

In front of me
pulled me, as a magnet.

It was littered with bone
of last eve's meal,
and dried carcass
of long dead creatures.

I cannot explain to you now
why I forged ahead.
My feet carried me to my destiny.

XVII.

It was then
I were caught
between that time of day ~

The dreadful hour.

Where light sleeps,
darkness invades,
and vision becomes
altered.

I swam to a rock, for safety.
Although I felt no fright.

For in this bend of my path,
I caught a glimpse
Of the flowing dark beauty

Which led me here.

XVIII.

Looking behind me,
I was stricken.

I knew I was lying in bed,
while lucidly dreaming
my raven.

I could see her, the woman.
My one true love.

Fallen by bedside,
knees, bruised.
Hands upon my brow,
weeping.

Her book was in my palm, now limp.

Beside the bed, a table
which stood a cup,
fashioned from maple.

I had crafted my own demise.

Once filled with love, such cup
where I drank of my mate.

Now brimmed with hemlock and nightshade.

When I drank of her words,
I drank of my death.

XVIV.

With each crack of twig,
I snapped back
to my blackened beauty.

She held her finger to my lips.

Sssshhhh... Come.

And I spoke not.

For my thoughts
were behind me.

My body lie
in the tears streaming
down the face of the woman.

My love.

I looked ahead, dazed
and parted lips to speak.
But had nothing of sense
to lend to this "diversion."

With salt upon my lips,
I held my hand to my chest.

Wishing to rid myself of the stone,
that had replaced my heart.

XX.

I then came upon a river.

To the south of me,
seething rapids spiked.

Each razor sharp tooth,
as that of a shark,
begged to bite of my skin.

And to the North,
serene.

Small ripples formed pools,
as damsel flies
graced its surface.

She stood between the two,
my raven.

A divider of time.

Her wings outstretched.
Brushing down upon each direction.

And she spoke:

XXI.

"What has befallen your home?"

My thoughts spun,
whorled by wintry eddy.

I fell beneath the South end of the river,
gasping and choking
for breath.

Then opened my eyes
to the depths of life.

I saw her, the woman
There she was, my love.

Sunlight streamed her crown, an aura.
Sending spikes of pure truth
from each knotted braid.

This penetration so deep
drove a flurry
of nails
into my skull.

And I saw a ship.

Looking to the sea,
I took flight
to the garden where we lay
before,
as three.

And my hands, once worn,
now made pure,
touched the face of my love
and she smiled.

Holding hands to her belly.

Yet her tears
melted this torrent realm
which I now housed.

I tried to swim to her.

She whispered beneath waves of glass,

"I loved you then, yet I was not the one."

She swam from me then.
Blond locks trailing
as that of a mermaids trunk
and left me, floating,
adrift.

I then spied her book.

XXII.

I snatched it quickly
held it to my chest,
clasping hands in prayer,

"Dear Father, I have been a foolish man.
I weep now for my faults, as a child to mother.
I hold within my possession, a sacrifice to you.
All I ask, in this dark hour,
Is that she find happiness."

Her words, once penned from tip of feather,
were now muddied,
mingled with brine.

Salt stung my face
becoming one with my tears
of horror.

I then felt myself
falling.

This life matters not.

I tried to be a good man
And have failed.

"My Creator, I beg of Thee, forgiveness.
But most importantly, I ask
to grant my woman
that which she has lost."

The water rushed in
and I welcomed the release.

XXIII.

After I found him,
seconds turned into a lifetime.

I sit here now, profile outlined
from the burning of the midnight lamp

I can still smell him on my palms...

Oh, how I loved him and always shall.

My failures caused his death,
and in my dreams, we meet.

As if it were that day, beneath the tree.

I recall my eyes, shining.
Watching him wield
axe and saw.

I retreat to slumber
thinking of him
with another
sound upon my breast.

XXIV.

Sleep had left me
and I paced the floor,
thoughts winding
counter clockwise.

Blue as the ocean deep,
hydrangea in bloom
fierce as fire
billowed as the summer sky…

I see them still,
his eyes.

Through the gaze of my mate.

I will not forget you, my love.
Even as I tread upon floors
of tiled stone
and light a fire
beneath hearth of ivory.

Each dance of flame
whispers your name.
My hand reaches out to you
only to be snapped back
by harsh burn of reality.

You will live on, my love.
I promise you this.

For the son we never bore
shall be proud.

And I shall call him,
Isaiah.

XXV.

Time had spun its web
apparent in lines, traced fine
beside each eye.

I find myself
tending garden.
Hands deep to wrist,
drenched with your body.

The rainfall, your blood.

You have seen me through winter.
Carrying my body through thicket and brush.

You have allowed me to love,
and be loved,
again.

My heart sings.

A lute
carried upon the breeze.

Yet, I am afraid, Lord.

It is almost time.

XXVI.

My thoughts wandered to the woman.
They always do.

And she held me then,
my black winged beauty.
Brushing locks of carbon
from my sight.

We stayed as so
an eternity.
Suspended within
the embrace of the river.

It had ceased raging eons ago.

I knew I had a choice,
yet my heart was not ready.

She placed her feathered palms
upon each side of my face.
Her breath, trailed, as a bubble.

I wanted to grab it,
take hold of it.

I knew if I did,
I would need to leave her then.

And when that bubble did burst,
her voice echoed,
warbled and wet,

"It is time..."

XXVII.

I embarked upon plank boards.

Palms sweating
with every tap of boot,
heel to toe.

I did not know where I was going.
I only knew
that I was now
but dust and ash.

And no longer was I frightened.

I felt weightless and free

My dark beauty, my guide,
has led me through the forest
past quicksand.

Into her arms.

And now, upon this ship,
my last remembrance
is looking back, seeing her waving.
Hair whipping in the wind,
onshore.

I turned then
and gave myself to the sea.

XXVIII.

It is time…

And I lie here
writhing in agony.

Midwife between my legs,
splayed to the heavens.

Oh, yes it was time,
and I secretly swore to Eve
for the curse of the pain I now felt.

With each rush of fire beneath,
my back arched and I screeched.

Tears flowing from each side of my face,
wet the cloth, pristine,
beneath me.

I swore to the sky
with each gasp of breath
and wave of anguish.

And pushed forth from me,
all that lies beneath the ground
and flies within the sky.

I pushed forth the stars and with it, the moon.

When I screamed, I was heard on high
and the angels joined me in choir.

A song of life

And when I had expelled
all of my prejudices,
my disdain and failures,
I then sat up and heaved forth
every needle pinch to skin
and each bleed of my heart.

When I opened my mouth
with head held back
as that of a woman, crazed

I heard him wail…

And I then let out my breath
and fell back, destroyed.

My only son.

I held our creation to my chest,
thinking of my one true love.

And he cried, my son,
as I held him in front of me.

A lone tear escaped
from breath, caught…

Isaiah stare back at me
with eyes,

Blue as the ocean deep,
hydrangea in bloom
fierce as fire
billowed as the summer sky…

I held him to my heart and cried.

For I knew he had been sent.

And we slept.

I, as a woman,
content.

Printed in the United States
62542LVS00004B/394-411

9 781424 119127